School with No Windows: Through My Lens

By Edward Gaston

MOzelle,inc.

Dedicated to Cheryl Quarles-Gaston
and the Carter G Woodson Elementary School
team and students,
past, present, and future recruits.

Copyright 2014 © Edward Gaston
MozelleInc.
Jacksonville, Florida

Library of Congress Control Number: 2014920624

ISBN 10: 9780692335246

THE NEW SCHOOL

In this age of smart phones and data plans, my phone makes a special sound when a new text message is received. On this particular summer day, the sound notified me of a multimedia text. The text read, *Picture from Stroy*. Above the text was a picture of a bathroom toilet that looked as if it had been sitting in an abandoned home for years.

Another text came through with the words, *And that is one of the good ones. This is my new school!* At the sight of that text, I knew there was a chance that things would not turn out well. Cheryl had pulled up a low-performing school in her first stint as a principal, and the school system decided she could do the same at a new school. But, as her husband and a strong supporter of her efforts to educate children, I was not sure if this was a promotion or demotion.

I took it as my responsibility to always check her school neighborhood to make sure that she would have a minimum amount of community support.

As an involved and known community development professional, it was simple for me to take on this role. I would make contact with other community organizations and encourage them to join my nonprofit, Wealth Watchers of Florida, in our support of Cheryl's new school. But, there was something different about this school, something that made me feel like it was going to be a long walk. It could have been the subpar F grade, the uncut grass, the unpainted exterior walls, the deferred maintenance, or the simple fact that the school did not have windows. It simply blew my mind that my wife was being recognized for her hard work in pulling up a school by being promoted to a school with no windows. How do you teach in a school with no windows?

Each night at dinner, the topic of discussion was Carter G. Woodson Elementary School and how to make a dollar out of fifteen cents. As the discussions continued, I arrived at one conclusion: Cheryl would not go down without a fight. If Carter G. Woodson Elementary School was now her blighted burden, she would fight to make it something more.

THE CHALLENGE

Dinner was generally our time to talk about our beautiful daughter. Together, we would daydream of everything she would become. We both vowed that no matter what, we would have major impacts on her life individually and as a strong parental team. But, now there was a new school that offered a huge challenge for my wife. This would be her second underperforming school—and the stress would be high.

Carter G. Woodson Elementary School was a sub F school and her assignment from the Duval School Superintendent was to pull the school up from the ashes. Cheryl sat across from me and said that she would accept the assignment with conditions. I was proud of her confidence. She understood that she had a say in her career and would not be set up to fail. Cheryl is extremely competitive and did not want anyone to label her as a failure based on a weak fight.

She explained that after she toured her new school for the first time, she immediately knew that she needed a team, a real team that would address real problems. She told me that she would not allow the normal way of thinking to stand in her way of trying to make a difference in the school. She was genuine when she said it would be all about the children, but, I also knew that she had something to prove.

She explained to the superintendent that she had one condition for accepting the position. She requested to take a team from her current school to the new one. The superintendent accepted her request, but, was surprised to hear her first choice was the head custodian, Stroy. Cheryl knew how important the environment of the school would be for improving learning and Stroy had received awards for the cleanest school.

SCHOOL BEGINS

It was the beginning of her first year at Carter G. Woodson Elementary School and Cheryl and her small team were the new kids on the block. Some of the remaining teachers who worked under the last principal seemed to still have an allegiance to a man who had not gotten the job done. The school had consistently scored Ds and Fs and did not show gains for the children—or even for the teachers.

Cheryl met with the entire school staff and made certain to communicate her goal of moving Carter G. Woodson forward. Cheryl advised everyone that it would be all about the children.

During her first months of leading the school, she received the most resistance from teachers who did not want change. They did not want change in leadership, change in style, or change in growth. They were just fine with business as usual and they had some union language backing them up. But, Cheryl having participated heavily in the union during her years as a teacher was knowledgeable and well connected. She knew that at the end of the day, the union cared more about the education of the child than assisting a couple of teachers with an uprising to make life difficult for the new principal.

She focused and took the time to review the knowledge, skills, and abilities of each one of her teachers. She was pleasantly surprised to discover that most of her teachers were on point. She believed only a few of them were not built to handle the daily demand of teaching a population of students where a 100 percent received free or reduced lunch.

Instead of dismissing poor teachers, each teacher was given the option to submit their paperwork requesting transfers. Cheryl gently opened the door and said no one would be looked upon in a negative manner if they chose to leave. For those teachers that chose to stay, she let them know that the journey would be long and hard.

As a result, some good and bad teachers stayed and some good and bad teachers left, which forced Cheryl and her management team to make more hard decisions. The bad teachers who chose to stay and try to inject negativity in the transformation process were identified and provided with an opportunity to improve or strongly encouraged to pursue positions elsewhere. In each decision, Cheryl and her team did not hesitate and she always ended our discussions after dinner and baby talk with, "It is all about the children."

PARENTS

You would think that Cheryl's initial concern would not be the parents. The school had been low performing for years, and the few active parents fell upon their lifelong conditioning of being loyal to whoever took care of their children and were not open to change.

Even though the last principal may not have delivered, many of the parents were loyal to him and did not know if they should embrace the new principal—a young, Black female who seemed more concerned with the cleanliness and appearance of the school than how many parents belonged to the PTA. Cheryl spoke to the parents in as many settings as she could. Sometimes she did all of the talking, sometimes the parents asked questions. After a few meetings with the parents, Cheryl discovered that there was not a PTA in place, providing another validation that her strategy and effort was focused in the right areas.

Through it all, Cheryl understood that the parents could not lead the charge—or truly embrace it—because they had never been exposed to a successful school. They did not know what to push for, how to push, why to push, nor for how long to push. From the meetings, Cheryl understood more than ever that at the end of the day, the children that she served had been placed in **her** care. It was up to her and her team to bring the necessary information, energy and guidance to the parents. For the first time, Cheryl saw directly and understood that it could not be just about the children. She now knew it had to be about the children and the family that loves and supports the children the best way that they can.

She needed a vacation early on but with a young daughter and new school to turn around, all she could do was go from home, to school, work some late nights, come home, and return back to school again.

CLOSING THE SCHOOL

The phone rang and it was Granddaddy Gigi. Cheryl's father was our link to the outside world. He ensured that we were informed regardless of our daily grind. My grind was working with a strong team of community development professionals to establish the foundation for a strong, sustainable nonprofit organization known as Wealth Watchers Inc. Our philosophy is, "If we are not assisting people, there is no need for us."

With that mindset, the Wealth Watchers team put in the time and helped stabilize many families during the mortgage crisis. Between the housing crisis and Cheryl's challenges at the school, she and I were in a constant grind. But we were smart enough to galvanize a loving network of family and close friends to help us manage our daughter's life of play dates, homework, dance classes, and recitals.

Cheryl and I did not read the paper daily but Granddaddy Gigi did, and the first thing out of his mouth when he telephoned was that the superintendent had Carter G. Woodson Elementary School listed for possible closure due to the low performance and enrollment.

Surely, they had not moved Cheryl to this school so that she could manage the closure. If so, they would have shown enough respect to inform Cheryl before putting it in the newspaper—wouldn't they?

Truth is, no, they wouldn't. As in many cases at that time, the principal and teachers were sometimes the last to know. Everything in the article made common sense, and Cheryl and I had to agree that Carter G. Woodson Elementary in its current condition should be on the list. I looked at Cheryl and I could tell immediately that it was a blow to her. It showed her that although the superintendent had selected her to lead the school, she wasn't untouchable. It gave her a clear view of the truth that her school and others were and always will be judged simply by the numbers. Those numbers—those achievement scores—impacted the entire community.

I learned from listening to Cheryl that the achievement scores of third grade students directly impact the community as a whole. Third graders! She told me the number of third graders with failing achievement scores on general tests is used to determine how many prison cells will be needed. An increase in third grade achievement meant a reduced need for prison cells. Poor performing third graders? Build more prison cells.

Cheryl and her team continued to approach each day aggressively. That is correct! Her team was very aggressive. They came together and made decisions as one band, one sound. Each time I visited the school, I could see progress taking shape throughout the school. But, I could tell that in the back of Cheryl's mind, she was waiting for the call from the superintendent saying it was time to close the doors. The team continued to push themselves and the students. They pushed the parents. And they pushed the district. The phone call never came.

NO WINDOWS

I was meeting with an architect who agreed to assist Wealth Watchers with developing a new apartment complex. He agreed to provide his work at a discounted rate and I accepted, telling him that his skills have always been needed in our community. From designing neighborhoods to designing schools, I gave him examples of how in low-income areas, roads, and zoning were scattered and chaotic and that some schools were constructed to resemble prisons. The architect, of course, came to the defense of his profession and stated that architects would not do such a thing. We went back and forth about specific neighborhoods and then we came to a tough spot on the designing-schools-like-prisons statement I'd made. He said it is not good to make statements without proof and that I should not just repeat what I had heard in the media. Of course, I told him that I had a baby at the house who controlled the day and I could not remember the last time I'd watched anything other than "Little Einsteins" or "Word Girl" on television.

After more debate, I told him that there is a school that was built with no windows and that I could direct him to it. He said that he would gladly make a trip to the school but that I needed to buy his airplane ticket. I laughed and said, "The school is less than fifteen minutes from us." He looked at me with a blank stare and went on to say that he does not know of one architect in our city that would design a school with no windows and that I must be mistaken. I gave him the address and told him to call me after visiting the school. Of course, after he left, it dawned on me that I had just sent an older white man to a school in the hood to walk around and look at it with no notice to the principal.

I tried unsuccessfully to reach Cheryl to let her know that she was going to have a visitor. Thirty minutes later, my cell phone rang, and it was the architect. "I don't understand how this could happen," he said. Even though he couldn't see me, I shrugged my shoulders and explained, "Sometimes there is a hiccup in our society and there is no one there with a clean glass of water."

That night, I asked Cheryl if she saw an older man walking around her campus outside. She looked at me with a blank stare and said, "Of course not, we don't have windows"

CLEANING HOUSE

Along with Cheryl and her team "cleaning house" by showing the door to staff who did not want to be there, Stroy, Cheryl's head custodian cleaned house in another way. Each time I visited the school it seemed as though it had received a new coat of paint. The hallways that were dull and soiled were now shiny and new. The oddly painted, dark walls, were now shouting at my eyes. Each time, I was able to see *and feel* a little more hope, a little more accountability, a little more pride.

And it did not end with the custodians and education team, the students understood what was happening and had bought into it. The students knew and understood that their environment was special and their legs, feet, and hands should not be placed on the walls. It was their way of showing pride and appreciation for the work that had been done to the school. Stroy made it a point to spend some weekends putting an extra coat of wax on the floor. Cheryl and her team knew that the learning environment was important and new paint and shiny floors were just the beginning. Stroy's crew understood what they had to do and made huge strides every day.

Cheryl knew she had the full support of the district and made the right calls to ensure that her children had a fair shot at the best learning environment possible. The floor tiles in kindergarten and first grade bathrooms that were stained and smelly were replaced. She requested and even demanded new desks and furniture for the students along with much needed items for the administrative office. Needless to say, Cheryl had created a name for herself with the district property maintenance department. She was not afraid to push for equity in her school and she constantly demanded what was fair.

When Cheryl discovered that her playground equipment and cafeteria tables were outdated and in desperate need of replacement, she and her staff pushed the district to replace and beautify the areas. The students responded with cheers and thank yous as she walked down the hall. A school that looked as though it needed to be shut down was now looking like a jewel.

STROY

Imagine a comedian who tells everything like it is. Now imagine a man respected by the entire school, staff, and children, who will do anything to help the school be successful. Roll all of that into a man who can make floors shine so that you can see yourself walking the halls. That man would be Carter G. Woodson Elementary School's Mr. Stroy.

He was known as Stroy. In fact, every faculty and staff at the school was called by just their last names. It was part of the unwritten culture there. Well, Stroy was the first person that Cheryl asked to take with her from her old school to her new one. The superintendent was so surprised with her request and he immediately agreed. Of course, Cheryl understood early on the importance of the environment and how Stroy would have an impact on creating and maintaining a positive learning environment daily.

Months after seeing the pictures of the deteriorated toilets and the grey halls, I visited the school to see freshly painted tan walls that brightened the school and the bathrooms were maintained on an aggressive schedule. Stroy and his team were experts at keeping a school clean. From the mark-free walls to the scuff-free floors, Stroy and his team had officially taken a school with deferred maintenance and transformed it into a quality elementary school ready for a 10-point military inspection.

Along with the overall maintenance of the school, Stroy also brought more to Cheryl's management team. He was yet another adult with words of wisdom and encouragement that the children admired. The students respected every adult on Cheryl's team from the custodian to the principal. The respect was mutual and required. This behavior reminds me of something Ralph Waldo Emerson said, "The secret in education lies in respecting the student." If an adult tells a child not to lean on the wall or to pick trash up off the floor, the child would comply.

If the child seemed out of character and the big brother told the secretary there was a household problem, a proactive approach was taken with the child, offering comfort with a hug and a reminder that they were connected to the pride of Carter G. Woodson Elementary School.

GOOD ENOUGH FOR BABY GIRL

After having our daughter in the classroom of Mrs. Harper, the best kindergarten teacher in the district, we were struggling with the decision on what school our daughter would attend for first grade. After a few weeks of her attending a neighborhood school, we quickly determined that we had made the wrong choice. So, we pulled her from the school and enrolled her in Carter G. Woodson.

We made the decision that our daughter would attend the school where her mother was the principal. First grade was a blur, but moving her to Carter G. Woodson Elementary with Cheryl was an excellent idea.

Our daughter provided Cheryl with insights from a student's point of view. She gave Cheryl information on everything—some observations were good, some were bad. But, in each case, Cheryl listened and made adjustments when possible. Our daughter chimed in on every possible need and want that the students had.

For example, she said students wanted more field trips, so, Cheryl built partnerships to ensure that students had excellent field trips. The playground equipment was very old, so Cheryl pressured the district and raised money to install new playground equipment with quality mulch. Our daughter really enjoyed her teachers. She understood that she was the daughter of the principal and that she had to represent us well. In the second grade at the age of seven, her teacher challenged the students to write their first book as a class assignment. With the help of a great illustrator and editor, my daughter's class assignment was converted into her first published book, e-book, and coloring book, *Summer Saves Summer*. At the age of eight, my daughter became a published author.

SEPARATE BUT EQUAL

Cheryl told me she was going to try something different with her fifth grade classes. She advised me that she would separate the boys from the girls, creating gender-based classrooms. Since I am not an educator, I had no idea of the basis behind the decision, but she seemed to be pretty sold on it. Of course, months later, I inquired about the benefits of the gender-based classrooms and Cheryl told me that everything was "going well." It was not until I later spoke to one of her team members that I discovered the actual benefits of gender-based classrooms.

Separating girls from boys was a huge success. The boys stopped acting out and the girls stopped showing out. And the classes became competitive with each other. The average test scores would be made available and the girls always wanted to score higher than the boys. Once the boys discovered that the girls were focused on scoring higher than them, as a class, they began working to score even higher than the girls. The competition caused both classes to increase their focus on education and achievement. The boys and girls never wanted their average score to be low, so good peer pressure was placed on all of the students—and even their teachers—

to do their very best. They even worked collectively to bring low performers up.

The gender-separate classroom helped to keep the students' behaviors above board. If a boy was underperforming or misbehaving, there was a constant and real threat that he may have to spend a week in the girl's classroom. And if a girl begins to lose her way with bad behavior, she knew that she may end up in the boy's classroom. The boys and the girls did not want to leave their team or let their classmates down. With the decision of gender-based classrooms, Cheryl and the teachers were able to creatively shift behavior and increase learning.

UNIFORMS

In addition to the fifth grade, gender-based classrooms, Cheryl decided that she wanted to improve the learning environment even more by requiring all students to wear uniforms. She received push back from some of the parents, but she still took the time to educate each parent on the benefits of school uniforms. Cheryl began speaking to parents who purchased the latest styles and brand names clothes every year for their children to attend school. But for some reason when the parents heard the word "uniform," they were conditioned to complain. Cheryl explained to the parents that uniforms would help to create a better learning environment and, in many cases, save money on school clothes. Even with that explanation, Cheryl still received resistance from the parents, with a few parents stating that they could not afford any clothes, let alone, polo shirts with the school logo on it. After hearing that, Cheryl began talking common sense with parents. She advised them that if they could not afford five shirts, they should just buy two shirts, washing them and hanging them up each night. I heard her tell parents on many occasions, "The education of your child is important and wearing uniforms will make a difference in how they see themselves and the understanding that education is worth wearing the uniform."

In addition to preaching to the parents, Cheryl had a secret weapon. She remembered that she had the most powerful weapons known for dealing with parents: their children. All Cheryl had to do was impress upon the students themselves that wearing a uniform is a good thing and they would do the rest. At that realization, Cheryl and her team started what I call Operation Treat for Uniforms. On certain days, each the week or so, Cheryl and her assistant principal would announce over the school intercom that it was time for the teachers to hand out treats to all students wearing their uniforms. The students did not want to be the odd person out so they bugged their parents to buy their uniform shirts with the Carter G. Woodson School crest embroidery. By the holiday break, the majority of the students were in uniforms daily.

And it did not end with the uniforms. One day, I visited the school to read to my daughter's class.

While I was reading, Cheryl came over the intercom and said, "It's Treat Time!" Right in unison, the children all stood up from their reading circle on the blanket, and made certain that their shirts were tucked in properly, and then returned to their crisscross- apple-sauce-hands-in-the-cookie-jar sitting position on the blanket and turned their attention back to me.

The teacher walked around the group looking at each student with approval and offered them a small bag of chips or piece of candy as their reward.

It simply was amazing how much self-pride they exhibited. It wasn't just them behaving to receive a treat. Those beautiful faces smiled with pride because they had done the right thing and had done it well. I was sold on the entire process.

AND TUTORING FOR ALL

Carter G. Woodson Elementary School was eligible to received funding that would allow the students to receive tutoring after school. Most people would think that tutoring is best used by students who were struggling or behind the curve. However, Cheryl and her team used tutoring not only to help struggling students but to reinforce excelling students. In order to achieve their vision of tutoring for all, Cheryl and her team went on a campaign to get the majority of the students to stay after school for tutoring. They sent notices home to the parents and kept instilling in them that this would help them all to be winners. For the most part, the students made the commitment to participate.

FUNERAL HOME SATURDAY

The school is located in an area of Jacksonville, Florida, that experiences some pretty rough activity. There have been shooting incidents in the area and in a few cases, the victim and assailant were somehow connected to one of Cheryl's students.

One day, prior to the start of the school year, she called my office phone to find me. I knew it had to be very important for her to call. Normally, she would text me or just wait until dinner to discuss her day. After answering the phone, she told me that she received a call from someone who wanted to be the school's business partner. You see, it is rare for any local business to call a public school in the hood and offer support. She went on to say she really did not know about the offer. We both agreed that this was a first. Then she told me the name of the company—A.B. Coleman Funeral Home. Yes, that is correct; a funeral home called Cheryl and offered their support.

We immediately had our radars up.

Was this funeral home trying to get its name out in the community as advertisement and benefit with more sales when someone in or near the school dies—or were they really sincere? Cheryl scheduled a meeting with the funeral home and asked that I attend. It seems that in her phone conversation with the funeral home representative, she mentioned that I was in community development and that I should attend and offer insight.

On that Friday at noon, we first met A.B. Coleman, owner of the funeral home. He explained that he was tired of burying people younger than twenty-five and that he believed that education was the only thing that could help change that. He went on to say that he would do whatever he could to help Cheryl make the school successful.

During the meeting, he asked what area could he have a huge impact. Cheryl thought about the question and said the school needed to have a flawless opening. Having a flawless opening meant that Cheryl would have more than 80 percent of her enrolled students show up on the first day of school.

Now, I know what you are thinking, *why is it an issue for children showing up for school on the first day*? Well, for some strange reason, parents began thinking that it was okay to not have their children present the first week of school, or the parents would wait until school started to complete important paperwork where enrollment forms were blank or the child's medical history was unknown. There have even been some cases when children did not attend the first days of school because the parent had not purchase clothes yet.

A.B. Coleman loved the idea and so did I. Cheryl and her team called it the "Carter G Woodson Elementary School Community Day sponsored by A.B. Coleman Foundation." They made phone calls and identified organizations including the health department, Shands Hospital, and other special community organizations to attend. Cheryl even invited Wealth Watchers to attend and of course, we accepted the invitation.

The Community Day took place on the Saturday before the first day of school. All of the students on record were called, but of course, many phone numbers were disconnected. So Cheryl had to go back to the basics. She made flyers and put them in all of the local businesses, including churches and the corner store that sold beer and crabs. She put flyers in beauty salons and she dressed up her marquee in front of her school announcing the community day event. She made sure that word got out that there would be games, bounce houses, free food, drinks, and several community resources to help every family.

On the day of the event, I set up my table early and was happy that I did so. The school was full of parents and children. Cheryl and her team had an excellent system. In order to make sure that each family received information that would help them, each parent was given a form that they had to have stamped by each vendor. Organizations were helping families pay utility bills, getting children signed up for scholarships, and conducting serious health screenings for the parents.

The event was a huge success. In the middle of it all was Mr. A. B. Coleman with the check available to cover all expenses, and the students showed up for the first day.

From that point on, A.B. Coleman became a rock supporter for Carter G. Woodson. He did special things for the children and the staff and tells everyone that he really is a Carter G Woodson Elementary School fan.

FAMILY REUNION

With a little girl growing, Cheryl and I agreed that we would attend family reunions on both sides of the family. We would connect with our families and give our daughter a chance to meet all of her cousins. My family reunions were in Birmingham, Alabama, and Cheryl's reunion took us back to Kentucky. We spent our Fourth of July in Kentucky eating mutton and listening to old family stories.

At this gathering, a special presentation was made highlighting a family member's contribution to the civil rights era. On the large projection screen, was an image of Cheryl's Uncle John being dragged from the front of the school board where he was protesting for more quality schools? Seeing Uncle John in that capacity came as a huge surprise to both of us and some other family members, too. Growing up in Birmingham, I was always reminded of the contributions of my family to the Civil Rights Movement to make things better for me, but I did not know that Cheryl had a champion in her family, too. We knew Uncle John only as a loving retired, high-ranking government official who had met every United States president for the last thirty years. Uncle John was an easy-going, calm man who gave our little girl her first fire-engine red tricycle. He and his youngest son, Joel, never missed a holiday meal with us, and they both made sure to clean their plates just to satisfy Cheryl.

Then, before our very eyes, we were viewing a photo showing a scrappy, younger Uncle John doing battle with the establishment to ensure that we had a better future. Cheryl was captivated with what she was hearing and seeing. I saw the pride in her eyes grow along with the rest of the family.

The screen highlighted an old article. We all stared, reading the words,

The pickets had not attempted a "lie-in" as The Recorder *went to press. Earlier this week, CORE served notice on the Board of School Commissioners that it was going to continue its protest "to impress upon you (the board) that CORE means business." The organization, in a one-page statement, told the board that if action was not taken soon, "frustration here might cause violence to erupt." They said that recent riots in Harlem, Rochester and New Jersey were caused by frustration of Negroes due to de facto segregation.*

The local branch of the NAACP also was represented at the school board meeting and said it was "less than happy at the efforts or lack of the same previous boards." The NAACP statement was far less strongly worded than that of CORE.

Meanwhile, the cases against three CORE members arrested July 30 during a sit-in at the School Board Building were continued until Aug. 27 in Municipal Court 3. The three, John Torian, Alfonzo Black, and James Pond, are charged with unlawful assembly in a public place.

As more information was presented, the entire family applauded and stood with pride, and Uncle John (John Torian) sat very humble with a smile. He understood the courage he'd shown throughout his life and was okay with us all knowing the truth. Uncle John and Joel continued to join us for every holiday event and special occasion. They continued to eat Cheryl's food, no matter the meal, and Uncle John remained his humble, easygoing, courageous self.

Cheryl, on the other hand, gave me the task of looking up Uncle John on the Internet, downloading pictures of him from his civil rights days and printing them out. She chose a picture of Uncle John being dragged from in front of the Indianapolis School Board, framed it, and placed it proudly on her desk in her office. It would send the perfect message to all who entered her office of her history and what she was willing to do to educate children with excellence and equity.

DOUGHNUTS WITH DAD

I have been pretty involved in the school since my wife is principal and my daughter attends the school. I try my best to attend every event and support anything dealing with student success. I have attended plays, choir performances, cheerleading competitions and school dances, all in support of the children. To my surprise, one day, my daughter tells me that she is inviting me to her school to have breakfast with her. She said that Doughnuts with Dad Day was coming up and that I needed to adjust my calendar to make sure that I am there with her. She said all fathers of the students were invited. I talked to Cheryl and she said her staff thought Doughnuts with Dad Day would be a great way to tie positive male role models to the lives of their students.

When my daughter and I arrived to the school on the special Doughnuts with Dad Day, the entire hallway was full of men. The hallways were packed and the students stood quietly. It took my breath away and a prideful smile came across my face as we all waited for the cafeteria to open. When the doors opened, smiling teachers directed us in to sit. And to my delight, all of the seats were taken and older students scrambled to get more chairs from other rooms.

Although it was billed as Doughnuts with Dads Day, we were served much more than that by four beautiful teachers. We all enjoyed a hot, hearty breakfast with our children, and we dads were in elementary school heaven. Every now and then I could see a mother trying to stick her head in to see the massive room of men, but, in each case a teacher would sternly turn them away saying that this event is for the men only. Cheryl wanted the fathers and male guardians to feel comfortable with interacting with their children at school. Although, we were from all different walks of life, each of us could recognize that we were being treated like kings. Then, Cheryl took the microphone and thanked the teachers who planned the event and went on to thank the dads, older brothers, step-fathers, uncles, and grandfathers for showing support and love for the students. And during her speech, Cheryl made one major observation. She said her hallways were full of students. In any other place and any other time, that many children in the hallway would be a formula for disaster, but, because there was a hallway full of men, the students were silent.

When the event ended, I knew that Cheryl and her team understood what they had accomplished. They had effectively silenced the stereotype that males do not make an impact. The impact of these males on that Doughnut with Dad Day was huge, positive, and well worth the effort of the men in attendance and the school team who pulled it off.

C++

For two years, Carter G. Woodson scored Cs on annual performance tests and showed exceptional gains for the students. Although, the school was still dealing with many of the same challenges, from high child mobility to major family ills, Cheryl and her team still believed that they could do better for the children.

She met with her team and spent many hours reviewing what had been done to bring the school from a low F to a C-plus. They wanted to know what they did right and what they were missing. And they ask themselves the question, "Is this all that our children can give?"

Each time Cheryl came home after one of those meetings, she seemed defeated. It seemed as if her team kept arriving at the same conclusion. Their children were doing everything that was asked of them and as they were instructed. They were giving their all and C-plus was the reality.

BOYFRIEND

I am a pretty confident person. Some call my confidence a good thing and some call it arrogance. I call it a damn good thing. If I don't believe in myself, how can I expect someone else to? And for this good thing called confidence, you can blame my parents and childhood friends for it. I grew up in an extremely competitive environment that required me to always give my best to keep up or to excel. Everyone could not play in the game; some of them had to sit on the bench. I did not like sitting on the bench, so I did my best to play in the game, give it everything I had, and to leave it all on the field. I say all of this to point out that I am not the most jealous man in the world, but, I was a little concern when I discovered that my wife had a new boyfriend and he was not this confident brother from Birmingham, Alabama.

Cheryl had key agencies outside her district that supported the school, teachers, and staff. Council for Educational Change, Partnership to Advance School

Success, and others provided funding and professional growth opportunities in the form of workshops, trainings, and continuing education for the staff. One of the agencies encouraged Cheryl to attend a special educational workshop.

After attending the workshop, she came home with a smile on her face a little too broad for a day at a workshop and said she had received some excellent information. Now, I attend many conferences per year and when I really get good information, I usually come back and try to share what I have learned with anyone who will listen. But, I can't remember a time when I came back from a workshop with a smile like the one Cheryl had. After telling me about the speaker, I noticed that Cheryl's smile seemed to widen on her face and there were pauses between her statements about his speech as if she was remembering every detail about him.

A few days later, she told me that she was called upon to do an impromptu speech about her most recent professional development workshop. She said that she began her update to her peers by mentioning the speaker's name, Pedro Noguera, and the fact that he was not only extremely knowledgeable but also "very easy on the eyes." And yes, she said this in a room mostly full of women.

There it was! Cheryl had a boyfriend.

She also had something even more—a potential solution to making her school better.

RAISING THE BAR

Cheryl was so excited about the man I called her new crush and the information he provided. It seems that Pedro Noguera offered educational insight that hit the mark with Carter G. Woodson Elementary School. One evening, she sat me down and asked me to listen. I was trying to watch a TED.COM video, but I saw the demand in her eyes, so I put my video on pause. She explained with great detail and passion that Pedro (that's right Pedro, he will not get Mr. Noguera out of me) spoke about changing the culture of schools and that educators should focus on the areas they can have the biggest impact. She told me that she spoke to her team and explained that she wanted them to start focusing on the things about the children that they can improve. She said that it was time to get out of the student's way and to stop discounting their potential based on their family circumstances. Cheryl's team agreed with her new way of thinking and simply started raising the expectation bar for every student. The children were expected to meet or exceed thresholds regardless of their personal background and circumstances. If the child was not at par, they were expected to attend tutoring to meet par. If the child was performing at par, then they were expected to attend tutoring to exceed par. If the child was exceeding par, the child was expected to attend tutoring to master the concept.

Each teacher and team member was reminded daily that the children were expected to perform in their studies. There was a total mindset shift in the school. The students knew what was expected of them and gave their all to do what they were being conditioned to do: EXCEL!

One clear example of this comes to mind when one day Cheryl came home with a big smile and shared a video with me. She discovered that her music teacher was really into the students and was on board with the new direction of the school. He used his music background and artistic gift to provide in-class and after-school music technology experiences for the students. He worked with the students and challenged them to write music, create lyrics, and film a music video. He led them in making two videos, "A's Up for Carter G" and "The Power of One."

Cheryl and her team applauded every teacher's extra effort with the students and this time the results were YouTube videos that created a great deal of pride for the students. Of course, that pride rolled over into the classroom and back into their homes. Cheryl understood that extracurricular activities were important for her students. She encouraged them to participate in music, sports, and other positive afterschool activities. She said it was important for them to develop the entire child, if Carter G. Woodson was going to be exceptional. I attended the showing of the video and heard the students talking about the music teacher. They all really admired him for leading them in developing musical art in a way that they were truly interested.

As I listened to one student speak about him, I was pleasantly surprised to find out that the teacher had a pretty strong musical background. It was said that he was a past drum major for the Bethune Cookman University Marching Band.

Not only was Cheryl pushing the students she also brought in teachers with exceptional talents and the courage to incorporate them in everyday lessons. Cheryl's teachers went above and beyond to add to the pride of the school. Teachers and staff coordinated excellent plays for the parents and community to attend, created music videos with the students highlighting the school, won citywide cheerleading competitions, and featured an award-winning choir.

Teachers, staff, and volunteers gave more to lead the school to awards and more school pride.

THE PHONE CALL

I really can't remember if I was out of town or if I was in the office. I think that I was out of town at a conference. Cheryl and her team had worked hard all year and were awaiting the school grade. Cheryl felt that her school had moved enough to make a B. She knew that they had left it all on the field and she was content with the effort of her team for the year.

Cheryl was raised by a protective mother and a Navy man, who is a real-life walking sports encyclopedia. And with that, Cheryl is the wife who sits down on a

Saturday during football season and sets the television reminder for every SEC game so that we won't miss a moment of action. Strangely enough, her favorite teams—Auburn University, my alma mater, and LSU—are both tigers and have very aggressive teams, which reminds me a lot of her.

After working half the day, I called her but I'd forgotten that it was the day they would find out the school's grade. When she answered the phone, I thought that I was on the phone with Cam Newton after the Auburn Tigers came from behind to beat the Crimson Tide and go on to win the SEC and National Championship.

Cheryl screamed in the phone, "We made an A!" Of course, being the daughter of a sailor, she screamed a few other words too. But, the basis of the communication was that after five years, hard work, dedication to children, support from beyond the district, and dynamic teachers and staff, Carter G Woodson Elementary School in Jacksonville, Florida, went from the lowest F school in the state to an A school! She had pulled off the impossible. The F school with no windows that was scheduled to be closed was now an A school with pride throughout the city of Jacksonville.

AFTER THE A

Everyone was extremely proud of the accomplishment of the students. Each person realized that they personally played a major role in the school succeeding. Even the students understood what they had achieved. The A status along with being approved to become medical magnet school made the school a beacon of hope and opportunity for the community and enrollment increased.

Cheryl came home one evening at the beginning of the school year still dancing on Cloud 9 and explained that she had been nominated by an unnamed person for the Lenard Miller Award as principal of the year for the State of Florida. Understanding and witnessing everything that she had done with her team to make it happen, we both took a moment to pause and reflect on the nomination.

The pause allowed Cheryl to embrace the pride that supporters felt toward her. Her mother and father were the overflowing with pride. Of course, they will tell you that they were proud of their youngest daughter, but, from my front row seat, I can tell you that they were overjoyed with her accomplishment. Not only has Cheryl made her parents beyond happy, she also represented well for Duval County because she, herself, was a product of the public school system and later graduated with a bachelor and master's degrees from the University of North Florida.

Everyone could find a reason to be excited for Cheryl because she did it the old fashion way: *she earned it with hard work.*

BABY AND COFFEE

My daughter is blessed with two sets of living grandparents. One set of grandparents is local and the other is in Alabama. She is the only grandchild on both sides and understands what is expected of her. To whom much is given, much is expected. The local grandparents—Grand Daddy and Grandma GiGi—are known for surprise gifts and brownies at the house, and the Birmingham grandparents—Feeshane and Bun Bun—are known for music lessons, drinking coffee, and making toasts to the future.

As we sat at the table with white linen, I watched my baby girl ask her mother for a cup of coffee. Yes, you heard me correctly, she saw everyone else drinking coffee and felt that she needed a cup of coffee too based on her mornings with Feeshane and Bun Bun.

After Cheryl fixed her a cream-based cup of coffee, two parts cream, one part coffee; my daughter began sipping on it like a little lady. I laughed as I turned the event program to the section with the full biography of Cheryl. We were in Miami with Cheryl so that she could be recognized as a recipient of the Leonard Miller Award, Principal of the Year.

When Cheryl rose to speak before the educators and community business leaders, my daughter raised her gaze from her coffee cup and began to clap for her mother with pride. I leaned over and asked her what she wanted to be when she grows up. My daughter looked at me and said, "First, I want to be a principal like momma and, then, I want to be a dancer." That was enough for me; I'll take it.

Cheryl's visibility and name recognition grew throughout the city and state. She and her team have received the following awards:

- 2012 Leonard Miller Principal Leadership Award
- 2013 Times Union EVE Award for Education
- 2013 NAACP Award for Education
- 2014 Youth at Risk Honorable Mention
- 2014 Solution Tree Redefining Excellence Award

Carter G. Woodson Elementary School continues to do well for the children even though, the students still have many of the same challenges and she has lost some of her best talent to other schools. That, though, is evidence of Cheryl's leadership abilities.

Her assistant principals are now principals of other schools, Reading coaches are assistant principals of other schools and new teachers have been brought onboard. Just like an SEC championship coach who loses star players to the NFL, Cheryl is constantly recruiting talented teachers and staff. She is always in a rebuilding stance. Through it all, Cheryl and her team took a school with no windows and an F performance grade to a medical magnet and A performance because they raised the bar for the children, the parents, and the community. Cheryl and I expected everyone connected to the students and the community to be involved. We expected everyone to reach and exceed the bar. And everyone involved rose to her expectations.

THROUGH MY LENS

I am not an educator and don't profess that this book is by any means a technical guide to improving schools.

Although, I am a product of a family of educators and my wife is an award-winning principal, this book is a recollection of events as told through the eyes of a common man who has never stepped in a classroom as a teacher or dealt with the ongoing educational demands of our youth. I am a community development professional who believes that the community support of schools lead to better lives and better business. I just wanted to put on record a story of a dynamic principal who focused on children and talented teachers with the aggressiveness of a hungry tigress looking to feed, protect, and shelter her cubs.

This is a story of a commitment to educational excellence. A story of a commitment to all children and their teachers. The story of Cheryl Quarles-Gaston and her elementary school educational team at Carter G

Woodson Elementary School in Jacksonville, Florida. In the previous fifty or so pages, I shared what I observed through my lens as a community development leader, a father, a son of educators, and a husband.

I continue.

Edward Gaston

By the way, if you really want to know the technical aspects of what happened to take an F school to an A, just look for Cheryl Quarles-Gaston on LinkedIn or Twitter. She loves children and believes passionately in education.

.

www.ingramcontent.com/pod-product-compliance
Lightning Source LLC
Chambersburg PA
CBHW020608030426
42337CB00013B/1277